A New Life Down Under

Jennifer Seidl

Cornelsen

Cornelsen English Library

Verlagsredaktion
Dr. Blanca-Maria Rudhart

Umschlaggestaltung
Heike Börner, dia

Titelbilder
Picture-alliance/Picture Press/Wartenberg, Frank P.
Corel Library

Illustration
Virginia Gray
Michael Fleischmann (Landkarte)

Fotos
Corel Library: Seite 12, 14, 22, 38, 39, 47, 49, 51
Autorin: Seite 12, 14, 24, 26, 39, 42, 46, 51, 59
Zefa/Corbis, Gary Bell: Seite 45

Typografie
Anna Bakalović und Annika Preyhs, Berlin

Technische Umsetzung
Ingo Ostermaier

www.cornelsen.de

1. Auflage, 4. Druck 2017

Alle Drucke dieser Auflage sind inhaltlich unverändert und können im Unterricht nebeneinander verwendet werden.

Druck: H. Heenemann, Berlin

ISBN 978-3-464-31780-8

PEFC/04-31-1156

PEFC zertifiziert
Dieses Produkt stammt aus nachhaltig bewirtschafteten Wäldern und kontrollierten Quellen.

www.pefc.de

Contents

Parts of this story are based on facts and true happenings at the Koala Hospital in Port Macquarie, New South Wales. Special thanks go to the supervisors and staff for their kind cooperation.

Chapter 1 Leaving

"Come on, Alice! Mum and dad are waiting for us," said Jeff to his sister as he checked his MP3 player and comics in his rucksack one last time. "Mum says the taxi will be here soon."

Alice looked round in her room once more. It looked so bare. All her clothes, books, photos, posters and her computer were no longer there. In fact, the whole house looked cold and empty. She felt sad. She didn't want to leave her home and her friends. Her dad was going to work in Australia for three years, so the family was going, too. But why so far away?

"The taxi's here!" shouted Mrs Clark from downstairs. "Come on now, Alice. We have to leave."

Alice had tears in her eyes, but she didn't let her family see that she was sad. Her brother Jeff was looking forward to Australia – he couldn't get there fast enough. Her dad, too. She remembered her father's words when he told them about his plans. "It will be a wonderful experience for us all."

Really ...? What was so wonderful about leaving your home and friends behind? Even her pet cat, Chico, lived with their neighbours now, and another family would live in their house for three years – or perhaps even longer? How could all that be so wonderful?

Alice was very quiet in the taxi on the way to Heathrow Airport. She looked out of the window. Everyday scenes of houses, shops, people with umbrellas, brown and white cows in the green fields were things she had never really looked at before. But now these things seemed very special to her – even the raindrops on the taxi window. It didn't rain much in Australia. She would keep these pictures in her mind and never forget them. It was her home … But Australia? That would never be her home.

*

The Cathay Pacific flight took off on time at 12.05. From her window seat Alice watched as the roads, houses and fields below became smaller and smaller, until they disappeared completely behind the clouds. Goodbye England … They would be in Hong Kong eleven hours later – or twelve, or more? Alice didn't know exactly how long the flight was, and it didn't interest her at the moment. But Jeff knew everything about the flight. He also knew lots about Hong Kong, where they would stop over for two days. His mum was looking forward to the old Bhuddist temples and the modern skyscrapers – an exciting mix of old and new side by side, she said. His dad was looking forward to the wonderful view of Hong Kong from Victoria Peak, and to real Chinese food. Jeff was looking forward to everything that was new and exciting. But not Alice.

"Right. Now listen and I'll read you some interesting info about Hong Kong," Jeff began enthusiastically.

"No, thanks," said Alice as she pushed her long, dark hair behind her ears and put on her headphones. "I want to watch the Mr Bean film." Alice wasn't really interested in the film, but for her it was a bit of England that she could hold on to for just a little longer.

She felt in her jacket pocket and took out her blue notebook. Telephone numbers, addresses, e-mail addresses and photos of all her friends were in there – and her favourite photo of Chico. She was homesick already …

"Well, then, I'll tell you all about Sydney," Jeff went on as he took a second guide book out of his rucksack. He began to read aloud: "Sydney is the capital city of New South Wales and Australia's oldest and largest city with a population of 4.2 million. Sydney is one of the most beautiful cities in the world with its harbour, ..." Jeff stopped suddenly. "Alice, you aren't listening, are you?" he said. "We're going to live there for three years – and you aren't even interested. Girls!"

Alice looked up at her brother. "I wonder what our cousins are like," she said to Jeff in a quiet voice. "I hope they'll like us."

"I hope we'll like *them*," said Jeff. "We've got to stay with them for a few weeks in Port Macquarie, until mum and dad have found us a house in Sydney, remember? Dad will be pleased to see his brother again after so many years. I expect Aunt Sarah is nice. Mum says she was in England with Uncle Bill and the kids ten years ago, but I can't remember her. Can you? We were too young. I'm sure our cousins are OK. Tom is 12 and Rachel is 14 or 15 now – just like us. Tom likes football and computer games, so he sounds all right. I hope he's got some good CDs and comics, and I hope I can watch his DVDs and play his computer games."

"Rachel likes horses. She can ride," continued Alice.

"Horses? Australia is famous for kangaroos and koalas. What about them?"

"Well, you can't *ride* kangaroos or koalas. But I expect Rachel likes them, too. I hope we'll see some."

"Oh, look. Here comes lunch. I'm hungry," said Jeff. "Are you having pasta or chicken? I could eat both."

"Jeff, don't be greedy! But I'm not very hungry, so you can have most of mine too."

"Oh. OK. And your orange juice? Yes? Great. It's a deal, sis."

After the meal and the Mr Bean film – and another meal and another film – they fell asleep.

They landed at Chek Lap Kok, Hong Kong's new international airport, on time. Jeff was very excited. He knew exactly how to get to the hotel from the airport. "We can go on the MTR. The Airport Express train only takes 23 minutes to Hong Kong Station. Then we can get a taxi to the hotel. It isn't far."

"MTR? What's that?" asked Alice.

"Well, it means Mass Transit Railway. It's something like the Tube in London, only better because it's new and clean and very fast," answered Jeff in his usual knowing manner. "I know because I read all about it yesterday in the guide book. But you didn't want to listen, remember?"

"All right, know-all!"

Jeff looked away and smiled to himself.

*

They all enjoyed the stopover in Hong Kong – even Alice managed to find some enthusiasm for the busy, colourful city. Jeff soon knew how to use the MTR and the Star Ferry and he exhausted the family with information about the sights. Alice wrote postcards to her friends. She also wrote them e-mails from an Internet café wishing them all a Happy New Year. She wondered if they were missing her ...

Chapter 2 A new country

"Next stop Sydney!" called Jim Clark just half an hour before landing. "Are you excited?" he asked Alice and Jeff. "I'm very excited, Dad. Are we nearly there?" smiled Jeff in his usual cheerful voice, as he pulled his favourite blue cap over his blond hair. "I bet I'll be the first to see a kangaroo!"
"Not at the airport you won't, stupid! I'm tired," complained Alice as she pushed back her hair from her forehead. "At home it's time to go to bed, and here it's time to get up. What time is it in London now, Jeff? I expect you know."
"Well, in Sydney we've got EST – that's Eastern Standard Time. From October to March when it's 7 am in London it's 6 pm in Sydney. So you can work it out for yourself now," replied Jeff, who couldn't be bothered to do maths puzzles so early in the morning.
"I'm too tired," said Alice, who didn't really care what time it was. But she was starting to feel just a little more interested in Australia now. She had no choice ...
What would Australia be like? Would they be happy in their new home – and at their new school? Would they make new friends? Would they feel at home in a hot, dry country, where the world's ten most dangerous animals were also at home – poisonous snakes and spiders, deadly jellyfish, sharks and crocodiles ...?
Ugh! Why did they have to go there, thought Alice.

*

"Wow, it's hot, even at seven o'clock in the morning!" said Mrs Clark about an hour later, as they left the airport building and looked for their rent-a-car on the car park. "But it's nice to see the sun so early, isn't it? You can't get sunburnt in London at seven o'clock in the morning."

"Well, it's winter in Europe, but here it's summer. It's very hot in the outback. But where we're going on the east coast it doesn't usually get hotter than about 30 degrees C. And the lowest average daytime temperature is about 15 degrees C. It has the best climate in Australia and there are some great beaches. I think Lighthouse Beach is one of the best," answered Jeff. "How far is it to Port Macquarie, Dad, and when will we get there?"

"I'm surprised you don't know, Jeff. You seem to know everything else," said Alice, hot and thirsty and not in her best mood.

"All right, you two. That's enough. Port Macquarie is about half way between Sydney and Brisbane, 400 kilometres north of Sydney. It will take us about six hours, longer if we stop for lunch and drinks on the way and look at the scenery. It depends on the traffic, too. Remember, it's the summer holidays here, so there will be more traffic on the road than usual. Come on, then. Everybody help, please. We have to get all these suitcases and bags into the car somehow. I think we're going to have a problem. I'll go and phone Bill to tell him that we've arrived. I won't be long. Look at the map, please, Maggie, and find out how we get to the Pacific Highway from here. At least the Australians drive on the same side of the road as we do, don't they?"

"It might be a good idea to find out, Dad ... " said Jeff with a roguish smile.

"Mum, put on the air conditioning, please, or I'll die of heat. Why does it have to be so hot here?" moaned Alice, taking out her bottle of water from her travel bag.

"Stop complaining, Alice. All you do is moan! I don't think it's too hot. It's certainly better than the cold, rainy weather we had in London. When can we go for some breakfast, Mum?" asked Jeff as he took the remains of a runny bar of chocolate out of his rucksack and licked it from the silver paper. "Well, now I've had some hot chocolate for breakfast," he said, licking his fingers, "but a couple of cheeseburgers wouldn't be bad either."

Twenty minutes later Jim Clark came back to the car with a plastic bag full of sandwiches and drinks. "I've spoken to Bill and Sarah," he said. "Everybody's fine. Bill said Rachel and Tom can't wait to see Alice and Jeff. Sarah said the kids didn't sleep much last night because they were so excited about meeting their English cousins."

"Well, we aren't very exciting," said Alice. "I hope they won't be disappointed."

"You mean, *you* aren't very exciting. Speak for yourself! I know lots of funny jokes, I can do card tricks, I love sport, TV and computers ..."

"You talk too much, and nobody likes know-alls," answered Alice. "So just be quiet, Jeff!"

"All right, that's enough, you two," said Mr Clark. "Let's eat our sandwiches and then we'll try to get straight onto the Pacific Highway. Port Macquarie, here we come!"

"But we want to see the sights in Sydney first," said Jeff with a cheese and tomato sandwich in one hand and a carton of orange juice in the other "The Opera House, Bondi Beach and Sydney Harbour Bridge. I want to do the Bridge Climb. Then I can tell my friends back home about it. They'll be green with envy."

"But not now, Jeff. We'll have plenty of time to see Sydney when we live there. We're all tired and we have to get to Uncle Bill's in Port Macquarie today. It's quite a long way and we don't know how much traffic there will be," answered Jim Clark.

"You two can sleep on the way, and I'll read the map for dad," added Maggie Clark. "I hope we don't get lost ..."

Driving in the morning city traffic wasn't easy – and unfortunately they got lost three times before they found the Pacific Highway. In fact, they saw quite a lot of Sydney and its surroundings ... Mr Clark was in a bad mood. He said sarcastically, "We've got three years to see Australia, Maggie. We really don't need to see it all today ...!"

Alice and Jeff looked at each other and chuckled quietly.

*

"Where are we?" asked a sleepy voice from the back seat a few hours later. "I'm hot and thirsty. Aren't we there yet?" Jeff asked as he took his cap from his face and scratched his head.

"Won't be long now, Jeff. We've had two stops at rest areas, but we let you sleep. We've seen some interesting things on the way – eucalyptus forests, where all the trees are black from the bushfires."

"Bushfires? Are we going to see some bushfires? That would be something really exciting to write home about," said Jeff, suddenly feeling more awake.

"Well, I don't think bushfires are very exciting, Jeff. They do a lot of damage and they can be very dangerous. Every year people lose their homes through bushfires, and lots of animals die in the smoke or are burnt," added Alice in a very serious tone of voice.

"How do bushfires start, Dad?" Jeff wanted to know. "I didn't have time to read about bushfires before we left."

"Well, I'm sure Bill and Sarah will tell you plenty about that," commented Jim Clark. "There aren't many summers in Australia without bushfires."

"We've seen several road signs to lakes, beaches and animal parks on the way," said Maggie Clark. "There's so much to see and do here. I'm quite excited about our new country. I'm sure we'll like it here. Look out for koalas. There were lots of warning signs. We may see some from the road."

"Any kangaroos?" asked Jeff, now fully awake.

"No, not yet. But there were lots of kangaroo warning signs, too. So they must hop across the road sometimes. Hey, look! Port Macquarie 15," said Mr Clark. "We have to leave the

Pacific Highway soon, then it's about another ten kilometres, on the Hastings River. So look out for the sign, everybody! Won't be long now. I hope Bill has got a nice cool beer in the fridge."

"And I hope Tom has got his computer on," added Jeff.

Chapter 3 The arrival

"Look! That must be it. Number 152. We're here!" shouted Jeff in an excited voice. "Wow! What a big house they've got!"

As they drove up to the front door, four smiling faces came out to greet them. The welcome was very hearty, with New-Year-wishes to add to the excitement.

"Uncle Bill, you talk just like the Aussies," was Jeff's first comment.

"Do I now? Well, I guess that's what it's like when you live here. You just wait, young man, next year at this time you'll all be talking like fair dinkum Aussies."

"I don't think so," thought Alice.

"What are fair dinkum Aussies, Uncle Bill?" Jeff wanted to know.

"Oh, it just means genuine, true Australians, Jeff," was the answer.

The girls were a bit quiet at first as they looked at each other and just smiled, but soon there was lots ot talk about: the flights, New Year's Day in Hong Kong, the journey up to Port Macquarie, how tired everybody was, how hot it was compared with London, and how good the cool lemonade was. Jeff was also very keen to hear what presents Tom had got for Christmas. The new computer game sounded very promising ...

"This is a great house," said Jeff in his usual loud voice as they sat at the table and enjoyed more lemonade and Aunt Sarah's home-made cookies. "So much space! We don't have this much space in Hampstead. It must have cost a lot. Do you earn a lot of money, Uncle Bill?"

"Shhh! You don't ask things like that," Alice whispered to her brother as she gave him a black look and kicked his leg under the table. "Why are you always so nosy?"

"Well, let's say houses here aren't quite as expensive as houses in London, especially in the Hampstead area," Bill answered with a laugh.

"Come, on, we'll show you your rooms," said Rachel to Alice with a friendly smile as she led the way upstairs with Tom. "Our parents have got lots to talk about anyway. They won't miss us."

"This is your room, Jeff, next to Tom's. It hasn't got a computer, but I'm sure you can use Tom's. This is my room, and this one is for you, Alice," said Rachel as she took Alice's hand, opened the door and led her into a bright, cosy room with a nice view. I hope you'll feel at home here." Alice smiled at Rachel and said quietly, "Thanks. It's lovely."

Tom was busy showing Jeff his room now. Jeff was particularly interested in Tom's DVDs and computer games, which were stacked neatly on a shelf. Tom's school books were also stacked neatly on his desk and on the shelves above his desk, but Jeff wasn't much interested in those. Tom had lots of books about animals, detective stories and adventure stories, which were much more interesting. He also had some magazines about cars and fast bikes. There were lots of posters of footballers on his walls, a collection of model ships on a shelf, and a football under his bed. "Mmm. I think I'm going to like it here," thought Jeff, "even though everything is neat and tidy."

There was a box on the top shelf which looked rather interesting, too. It was a bit longer than a shoe box perhaps, and a bit deeper, and tied up with a piece of string. In his usual curious manner Jeff asked Tom what was in the box.

"Oh, nothing much," answered Tom after a pause. "It's private."

Jeff was curious, of course. He loved secrets and private things – especially if they were someone else's – but just then Rachel and Alice burst into Tom's room.

"Come on you two. Let's help Uncle Jim to unload the bags and bring them up," said Rachel, who in her resolute manner liked to tell her younger brother what to do. So they all went downstairs, helped themselves to another glass of lemonade and then helped with the bags.

"It's so hot here. It was raining in London when we left home," Alice told Rachel half way up the stairs, carrying a heavy suitcase and her travel bag over her shoulder.

"Well, doesn't it always rain in England?" asked Rachel with a smile. "You're lucky. We'd love to have more rain here. Visitors from Europe always think our Australian sun is fantastic, but we're glad when it rains."

"Erm ... Rachel, do you think I could use your computer to write to my friends back in London?" asked Alice, changing the subject. "Just to let them know we've got here safely?"

"Sure, no worries," answered Rachel cheerfully. "I'll show you my computer. You can use it as often as you want. Just ask me if you need any help. You're going to meet some of *our* friends and neighbours tomorrow. Mum and dad have organised a big barbecue before your parents drive back to Sydney. Some of my friends are coming and some of Tom's friends, too. They're coming to see *you*. They're all very curious about our English cousins. My best friend Shannon has already called three times to ask if you've arrived. Trish and Jane, too. They're all in my class at school. You'll like them, you'll see."

Alice didn't answer. The idea of lots of people coming especially to see them made her feel uncomfortable. She was quite a shy, sensitive girl who didn't make friends easily. She didn't want to be on show. In fact, the idea of tomorrow's barbecue didn't please her much at all. So many new people. She wasn't outgoing like Jeff, who was always direct and self-confident. He would go up to people and joke with them as if he had known them all his life. He was robust, energetic and outspoken. He liked to play the clown and be everybody's favourite. But not Alice. She was gentle, sensitive and often serious. Little things meant more to her than they did to Jeff. She valued things more, especially friendships – and she got hurt more easily. Tears filled her eyes when she thought about Chico. He had been a hungry stray, and Alice had taken him home. There was a special bond between them. Were the neighbours treating him with as much love as he deserved? Was he missing her as much as she was missing him? She was missing her friends back home, too, but she didn't speak about it. She didn't want the others to notice. She wrote e-mails to Ann and Lucy before she went to bed, then she lay awake thinking all kinds of melancholy thoughts.

However, the excitement of the day with all its new impressions had made Jeff and Alice tired. Alice fell asleep at last, and she slept soundly in spite of the sad thoughts of home. Maybe she would get e-mails back from her friends in the morning. She tried not to think about tomorrow's barbecue – that would come soon enough. Tomorrow was another day …

Chapter 4 The first day

"Well, how do you like Australia, you guys?" Aunt Sarah asked Alice and Jeff at breakfast.

"Well, I think it's great here – and I know a lot about Australia from the Internet, Aunt Sarah. It's a pretty big country, 7.7 million square kilometres – that's 32 times bigger than the UK. It's the sixth largest country in the world. It has a population of about 20.5 million, but only about 1.9 per cent are Aboriginal people, and 94 per cent of the Australians were originally Europeans."

"Really, Jeff, I'm impressed. You have been doing your homework. You can tell us Aussies things we don't know," said Aunt Sarah with a smile as she brought toast and fresh bread rolls from the kitchen. "You even know about our Aboriginal population. That's great."

"Yes, they came from Asia about 40,000 years ago and they were the first inhabitants of Australia. The Europeans who moved to Australia gave them the name 'aboriginals'. It means something like 'people who have lived there since the earliest times'. Most of them live in cities now, but some still live in the traditional way, hunting in the bush with boomerangs. Can we go to the outback, Uncle Bill, and probably meet some Aboriginals? That would be very interesting."

"Well, it's a bit too hot in the outback at the moment, Jeff. That's a trip that you have to plan very carefully," said Uncle Bill. "We can't do it now, but I'm sure we can do it with your parents some time in the next three years. Maybe we could all go to Ayers Rock – that is to Uluru as it's called now, using the Aboriginal name – and Alice Springs. I know your dad would love to see the outback. It's a fantastic experience."

Uluru (Ayers Rock)

Aboriginal Cave Painting

Alice Springs

"Sure. Dad loves adventure – just like me," said Jeff enthusiastically. That would be really great, Uncle Bill."

"Well, after breakfast Bill is going to show you around our town," said Aunt Sarah. About 65,000 people live here in Port and its surroundings. It isn't quite as big as London, but you'll like it, you'll see," she continued.

Alice thought that she had heard those words somewhere before: *you'll like it, you'll see*. Everybody seemed to be so sure that she would like everything and everybody. After all, everything was so wonderful, wasn't it? Especially the heat, the dangerous outback and the deadly reptiles. Alice would like to have visited Australia for a few weeks, just on holiday, but she didn't want to live there for three years – or even longer. She suddenly felt very homesick. Somehow she felt quite sure that she would not be happy in the new country. Everybody was nice to her, but really they were all strangers – and she felt like a tourist ...

Jeff on the other hand was looking forward to meeting new people and to seeing everything that New South Wales had to offer. He had enjoyed every minute of his new life so far.

"Why can't I be more like my brother?" thought Alice, again in a sad mood, as she read the e-mails she had just received from her friends in London again and again. They had written about their Christmas holiday activities and they had said how much they were missing her.

"Come on, Alice. You aren't eating much. Have another roll with some of my home-made jam," said Aunt Sarah in a warm, motherly tone. She was kind, so Alice smiled and tried to look happy to please her. Just then Rachel's mobile rang. It was Shannon – again. Rachel went into the kitchen to talk to her.

"Well, I'd like to visit the Maritime Museum or the Billabong Wildlife Park," said Jeff, already planning the programme for the day. "But it's hot. Can't we go to the beach first?" he asked. "I know there are lots of beaches quite close. Town Beach, Flynns Beach – great for surfing, Lighthouse Beach, Nobbys Beach, Oxley Beach, Rocky Beach ... and erm ..."

"Hey, Jeff, you know more about Port than I do!" laughed Tom, obviously impressed by Jeff's detailed knowledge of his own home town.

"Or how about Lake Cathie for a great picnic place?" continued Jeff happily, encouraged by Tom's comment. "Or you could teach me to windsurf, Tom – at Big Bay, Pilot Beach, Trial Bay ... Or we could hire a boat and go fishing on the Hastings River."

"Hey, hey, slow down, Jeff!" interrupted Uncle Bill. "Remember, we're having a barbecue tonight and we have a lot to prepare, so we don't have much time to spare today. But we'll have plenty of time to do all the things you want in the next few weeks. That's a promise."

"OK, Uncle Bill. Perhaps Alice and I can help with the barbecue. I could sample all the food for Aunt Sarah."
"Jeff, don't be so cheeky! Think before you say such things!" said Alice in a quiet but very serious voice.
"Oh, come on, Al! She's our aunt. She must know it was just a joke. Calm down, big sis."
"And don't call me 'Al'. You know I don't like it." Alice was relieved that everybody else was chatting and nobody seemed to have heard their conversation. Alice loved her brother, but he could be a bit too direct sometimes.
"Well, come on then. I'll show you the sights," said Bill after breakfast, picking up his car keys from the hall table. "I know the best ice cream place in town. They have different flavours every day – and special big portions for hungry 12-year-old boys from London!"
"Great!" thought Jeff, who was always ready for an ice cream – even after a big breakfast. "I'm sure I'm going to like it here."

*

On their walk through the town, the Clarks saw several historic buildings including the Courthouse and St Thomas Church, some interesting gift shops and antique shops, besides a shopping mall. They bought sun hats and sunscreen for everybody. Uncle Bill explained that because of the ozone hole, you can still get sunburnt even when the sun isn't shining.
"We say 'slip, slop, slap' here. Do you know what that means, Jeff?" asked Tom trying on a large Mexican-looking hat and laughing at himself in a mirror. "That means 'slip on a shirt, slop on sunscreen and slap on a hat'. Every kid here knows that. The sun is very dangerous in this part of the

world. When we go to the beach you'll see the little kids wearing swim suits with long sleeves. We always wear T-shirts on the beach. And we never go at midday when it's hot, usually early mornings or evenings."

That was, indeed, something that Jeff didn't know.

"And you have to watch out for the stingers and sharks, too. They can kill you," said Tom to Jeff.

"Oh, I know what stingers are. They're box jellyfish. They're small and you don't see them because they're transparent, right?" added Jeff. "You can be dead within a few hours."

Alice heard what the boys said. She was sure that she would never go in the sea in Australia. "That can't happen to you on an English beach," she thought.

*

At home Aunt Sarah was busy preparing food for the barbecue, a real Aussie "barbie" of steaks, fish and salad, she had said. And lots of great desserts!

"There you are – at last! How was it?" called Sarah from the kitchen when the family arrived back home. The patio was now decorated with coloured lights, balloons and Chinese lanterns.

"Wow!" said Jeff when he saw the decorations. "We can't have garden parties back home in January."

"I've got jobs for everybody," Aunt Sarah continued before the kids were able to disappear upstairs. She soon had them all carrying chairs, plates and glasses and setting tables.

"You'll like my friends, Alice," said Rachel as they were carrying garden chairs out of the garage. They're good fun. Their names are Shannon, Trish and Jane. Shannon and I go riding together. You really must come and watch us some time. Maybe you could take some riding lessons, too."

"Yes, maybe," answered Alice without much enthusiasm. She wasn't keen on sports, and although she liked horses she had never had the chance to learn to ride back home.

"Well, I think we ought to get ready," said Sarah to Bill as she took off her kitchen apron. "The first guests will be arriving soon."

Why did Alice have an uncomfortable feeling in her stomach?

Chapter 5 The welcome barbecue

Alice was still in her room when the first guests arrived. She heard laughter and several happy voices from the garden below her window. Australian voices without faces. Strange that the laughter should make her feel nervous …

"Alice, come on! Where are you?" shouted Rachel up the stairs.

"I'm still here in my room," answered Alice. "I've just washed my hair and I can't get it to look good. And I feel so hot."

"I always wear my hair short for that reason," said Rachel, going into Alice's room. "Mmm. Well, we'll put your hair up, then it will be cooler. Just wait and I'll get some hair stuff from my room."

Alice didn't get the chance to protest. Rachel disappeared and reappeared with combs and different hairslides and was already designing a totally new hairstyle for her cousin.

"Right! There you are! I think it looks great. Come on down, I think I heard Shannon's voice," Rachel added with some excitement. "Come on! I'm dying to introduce you! She's great. She's the smartest in the class – and the best at sports. And she can have her pick of the boys."

Alice didn't comment. She looked in the mirror and hardly recognised herself. It wasn't the kind of hairstyle she would have chosen at all, but she couldn't tell Rachel that she thought her hair looked stupid. It made her feel cooler that way – but certainly not better. Jeff would be sure to make some stupid comment to embarrass her in front of all the guests.

She had put on a fresh white T-shirt and her best jeans – all rather conservative. She didn't use make-up apart from a bit of lip gloss. Her dad always said she was pretty enough without make-up. But then, that was her dad. Rachel's friends would most likely judge that differently.

Before she left her room, she took a silver cross on a chain from a small box in her suitcase. It was a present from her grandmother who had died just a year before. Her grandmother had said to her, "When you wear this I'll always be with you, and you need never be afraid." Alice put the chain round her neck.

"OK, Alice. Here goes!" she said to herself as she walked quietly down the stairs. She told herself that there was nothing to be nervous about, but she had butterflies in her stomach, just as she always had before a school test.

*

Somehow Rachel had disappeared, so Alice went into the kitchen first to see if she, Jeff or her parents were there. She didn't want to make her entrance to the party alone. But the kitchen was empty. Everybody was outside chatting. But not quite everybody …

"Oh, you must be Alice," said a young girl's voice suddenly from behind. "I'm Shannon, Rachel's best friend. Hi, and welcome to Port! Rachel has told me a lot about you. Do you like it here?"

So that was Shannon, the girl Rachel had called on her mobile at least six times. She was blond, slim and sporty, pretty, too, with perfect teeth and styled hair. She was outgoing, bubbly and self-confident. She wore trendy clothes, eye make-up and large earrings which looked good on her.

"Yes, I'm Alice," said a quiet voice, taken by surprise. "Hello, and yes, we all like it here. But I'm not used to the heat and the strong sun yet." She immediately thought that was a stupid thing to say, but it was the first thing that came into her head.

"Well, that's Australia. Sun, sand and surf. We've got plenty of all three. But we certainly don't complain. Our climate here is the best in the country. How long are you staying here?" Shannon wanted to know.

"Until our parents find us a place in Sydney," answered Alice.

"You mean a house. Surely you won't live in an apartment," Shannon replied. Alice thought that was a strange comment to make, but continued, "And we have to start our new school in Sydney after the holidays."

"Well, school starts at the end of January. If you're staying here until then, maybe we can do something together. We live just up the road, in the big house with the swimming pool and the tennis court. You can't miss it. Rache often comes for a swim, or we hit a few balls together. Then we hang around at the pool or in town. Sometimes my brother Cam brings his friends and we have a pool party. Anyway, where is Rache? I expect she's in the garden with the others. Come on and meet our friends. By the way, your hairstyle is cool. Different. Come on."

Alice didn't answer. She couldn't believe that Shannon's compliment was sincere, because she knew that her hair looked pretty stupid. But Alice followed her into the garden.

They soon found "Rache", who was serving cold drinks to all the guests. There must have been at least twenty people there already. When Rachel saw Alice, she said spontaneously in a loud voice, "Here she is. Everybody, this is my London cousin Alice!"

Suddenly all eyes were on Alice. That was the moment she had been fearing most. She felt herself go red in the face, but she smiled and said "Hi!" and people came up to her and started chatting. There were Trish and her brother Rob, Jane and her sister Mel, and the Jacksons from next door with their two teenage sons. Friends of Uncle Bill and Aunt Sarah's were talking to Alice's parents. Jeff was in the middle of the group of 12-year-olds, telling English jokes or asking how much homework you get in Australian schools, or some such stuff. He always found plenty to talk and laugh about. Several people said they liked to hear their English accent, so even Alice found herself talking more than usual.

*

The party went well. Uncle Bill even managed to set the barbecue on fire – much to the delight of Tom, Jeff and the other young boys, who found it exciting and highly amusing. Some of the steaks were very, very well done, Jeff commented.

Alice liked Trish, who seemed to be quiet and maybe a little conservative – like herself. Trish certainly wasn't like Shannon, who was the centre of every conversation. She seemed to draw people like magnets, especially the boys. You could always find Shannon in the middle of a group of boys, laughing and flirting. And she seemed to be the leader of the girls, too. Alice didn't like her, and she couldn't understand why Rachel did.

Just before the party came to an end, Shannon walked up to Alice and said, "My parents are going away tomorrow for a few days, so my brother and I are going to have a pool party. Maybe Tuesday. You can come if you want. There will be the usual crowd and some of Cam's friends, too. It's always great fun. But don't bring your little brother."

Alice thanked Shannon politely for the invitation, but she didn't feel too happy about it. And why wasn't Jeff invited? Alice had never been to a pool party before, and she hadn't met Shannon's brother either. Maybe he was just the same kind of person as his sister. Shannon was a born leader – and Alice didn't like to be led. Her friends Ann and Lucy back home weren't like that. They discussed things and decided things together. Nobody told the others what to do. Nobody was the leader. Alice had hoped that she would be able to spend lots of time with Rachel in the next few weeks, to get to know her cousin better. Maybe she would feel more at home if she had a good friend. But there wouldn't be much chance of that if Shannon was going to be around all the time... Alice thought that maybe she would be lonely in Port Macquarie after all.

On the next morning when her parents left to drive back to Sydney, Alice had tears in her eyes.

Chapter 6 Making friends

The next few days were full of new impressions for Alice and Jeff. Uncle Bill took time off work to show them around. They did a boat trip up the Hastings River. They visited the Sea Acres Rainforest Centre and did a guided boardwalk tour there. It was beautiful and cool under the canopy of green leaves. Of course they spent time in town and down at the marina, where they watched some jet-skiers. Aunt Sarah told them to visit the information centre and get street maps of the town – "just in case you get lost," she had said. Jeff enjoyed the Maritime Museum, but he enjoyed the meal at the Pancake Palace afterwards even more. He even had a camel ride along Lighthouse Beach. Nobody in his school class back home had ever done that.

On Tuesday evening, Rachel took Alice to Shannon's pool party. Alice wasn't looking forward to going, but she was curious. She had never seen a house with a swimming pool and a tennis court in London. It wasn't far, so they went by bike. Aunt Sarah had said that Alice could take her bicycle any time. Jeff stayed at home with Tom to play computer games, and Aunt Sarah and Uncle Bill were out.

When they arrived at Shannon's house Rachel rang the bell at the big front gates, which opened automatically. Alice noticed video cameras on top of the gates. The girls drove up the long drive and parked their bikes somewhere at the side of the house under the trees. Rachel noticed Alice's surprise at the big house and told her that Shannon's father owned a business, an IT company or something like that, and that he wasn't at home very much. Shannon's mother sometimes went with him on his business trips abroad, so the kids were often alone at home.

As the girls went round to the pool at the back of the house, loud music and laughing voices greeted them. There were coloured lights and lanterns everywhere in the garden, which was like a park. There was a water fountain and benches to sit on under the trees. The pool was lit up. The water glittered in a beautiful turquoise colour and looked so inviting. Some teenagers were sitting at the pool side, dangling their feet in the cool water. Others were swimming and splashing.

Shannon appeared in a stunning red and white beach outfit with a wrap-around skirt and sandals with high heels. Alice thought she looked much older than she was.

"Wow! So that's the outfit you told me about. You look great, Shannon – doesn't she, Alice?" asked Rachel, genuinely enthusiastic about Shannon's new clothes.

Shannon didn't wait for Alice's answer, she took Rachel and Alice by the arm and walked over to a group of girls standing by the pool. "Hey, guys, this is Alice," she said. "I'll join you later."

"Oh, you're the girl from London. Shannon told us about you. Well, come and join us. I'm Patty," said a girl with long, blond hair.

Patty and three others talked to Alice for a few minutes, then when Shannon joined the group the conversation turned to new clothes and make-up, new CDs and party invitations, and of course, boys. Alice thought the conversation was superficial and rather stupid. Was there really nothing more interesting to talk about? Why had she come to the silly party? Just then some boys came over and Shannon started chatting to them about surfing. They all laughed out loud at something that Shannon said. She was the centre of the group – as usual. Boys never gathered round Alice like that. She didn't have a boyfriend. The boys in her class at school were just friends. None of them was in any way special to her. She spent her free time reading. She was very interested in books on animals and environmental problems. She was good at art. She liked to draw and paint. She liked writing to her e-friends and spending time with Ann and Lucy. But boyfriends? Not yet.

Alice managed to leave Shannon and the group without anybody noticing. Then she saw Trish and Jane, who had just arrived and were helping themselves to orange juice. "Hi, Alice! Great that you've come. How are you doing? Come and tell us where you've been these last few days," Trish said in a cheerful voice. Jane said she would join them later.

Alice and Trish left the pool area, where the music was loud, and found somewhere quiet to sit under the trees. Alice told Trish where they had been and what they had seen and what they were planning for the days following. Alice felt comfortable with Trish. She was a bit like Ann and Lucy.

Just then a voice from the house shouted Trish's name. Trish looked towards the house, stood up and shouted, "I'm over here!" A good-looking 16-year-old boy with dark hair hurried to where Trish and Alice were sitting and said, "Hi, Trish. There's a call for you from your mom. She says you forgot your cell phone, so she called here. Can you call her back immediately? You can use the phone in the hall, OK?"

"Sure. OK," answered Trish. "Thanks, Cam. Alice, I'll be right back." Trish put down her glass and ran back to the house.

Cam? Had Trish said "Cam"? Was that Cameron, Shannon's brother? Alice hadn't met him before as he hadn't been at their barbecue. But then, why should he have been there? Shannon, not Cam, was Rachel's friend. Cam smiled at Alice and said, "Oh, so you're Alice, Rachel's cousin from London, aren't you? Hi, I'm Cameron, Shannon's brother. Do you

mind if I sit down until Trish gets back?" Alice was again taken by surprise.

Cameron was not only good-looking, he was polite and friendly, too. He told Alice that he had been in London for a year on a student exchange, and that he had loved every minute of it. He said he really liked the British and loved their country. He knew his way around London quite well, and they talked about lots of places that they both knew and liked. He had even flown a kite on Hampstead Heath, which was just a short walk away from where Alice lived – or used to live.

They talked very easily together about all kinds of things: music, hobbies, school, which countries they would like to see, what they might want to do after they left school. Cam said his dad would like him to take over the family business, but he would prefer to study something else, like medicine. He was even thinking about becoming a vet.

Alice found herself telling Cam that she was homesick. Cam replied that he could understand that because he had felt just the same way at the beginning of his stay in London. She told him how much she missed her cat Chico, and he told her about his pet dog Benny who had died not long before. Then she said they were going to Billabong Koala Park the next day, so he told her lots of really interesting things about Australian animals and birds: dingoes, wombats, wallabies, platypuses, possums, black swans. Alice had never heard of some of them: echidnas, Tasmanian devils, bandicoots, quokkas, cassowaries, kookaburras, bellbirds.

Cam was so interesting to talk to, really nice, not like Shannon.

"Oh, your glass is empty. Just a moment. I'll get you some more juice," Cameron said with a smile. He stood up and

Dingo

Palm Cockatoo

Pretty-face Wallaby with J

Cassowary

Kookaburra

Sulphur Crested Cockatoo

Rock Wallaby

took her glass. "Don't go away!" he said and hurried back up to the house. "I'll be right back."

Alice couldn't explain why, but when she saw Cam coming back to sit with her, with a glass of juice in his hand for her, she had butterflies in her stomach again, just as she always did before a school test. Only this time it was different somehow ...

"Turn the music up, Cam!" shouted one of the boys when they were sitting round the pool a little later. But Cam didn't turn up the music. He obviously thought it was quite loud enough. In fact, he seemed to be different from most of the others. He was quieter, more serious, more sensible. He wasn't smoking or drinking beer and he wasn't dancing around wildly or doing anything crazy like some of the others. He did what he wanted, not what the others wanted him to do. He was strong. Alice liked that. Yes, Cam was really nice.

When Rachel and Alice left for home, Cam rode with them – to make sure they got home safely, he said. Alice wondered if Cam always cycled home with Rachel. Maybe he did. Maybe he was just being polite. But maybe he didn't always cycle home with Rachel ... Alice didn't ask.

Just before Alice and Jeff went up to bed, their parents phoned from Sydney. There was lots to talk about. Their mum said they had found out where dad's new workplace would be and where the nearest high school in the area was. They had spent time looking at lots of houses, but they hadn't found one yet that would be ideal for all the family. Jeff didn't seem to care much about where they would live in Sydney and where they would go to school. At the moment Port Macquarie was much more interesting – for Alice, too ...

Chapter 7 A great day out

Today would be very special. Uncle Bill and Tom were going to take Alice and Jeff to the Billabong Koala and Wildlife Park, where there were over 50 different kinds of Australian animals, from cuddly koalas to poisonous snakes. Uncle Bill said there were daily shows where you could learn a lot about koalas from the animal keepers. You could pat them and take photographs, too. Alice had heard so much about koalas and kangaroos from Cam, and she was excited at the thought of seeing them for the first time. She hated snakes, but Jeff was looking forward to the new reptile house, of course.

It wasn't far to Billabong, just a few kilometres south. On the way there Jeff asked about bushfires. "How do bushfires start, Uncle Bill?"

"Well, South Australia has some of the worst bushfires in the world because of the extreme weather conditions we have here, high temperatures and very little rain. Everything is dry, so even a spark from a camp fire or a flash of lightning will be enough to start a fire. If there's a wind, you soon have a pretty big fire, especially if there's a lot of material that burns – like eucalyptus forests. The trees store oil in their leaves, so they burn easily and the fire spreads quickly from tree to tree. Suddenly a whole forest is on fire. And often there are several fires in different places all at the same time. Unfortunately, quite a lot of bushfires are started deliberately."

"How can people be so stupid?" said Jeff. "Don't they realise what they're doing and how dangerous it can be?"

"That's a very good question, Jeff," answered Tom. "Lots of animals get burnt, especially koalas because they live in the tops of the eucalyptus trees and they can't run away. Wombats are safer in fires because they live under the ground most of the time."

"That's right. We'll see some wombats in Billabong. They're really cute little fellows," added Uncle Bill. "They're the closest relatives of the koala, but they have bigger brains, so they're more intelligent and quick to learn. They spend two-thirds of their life under ground. They just come up for food, and they can

Wombat

walk long distances. They can even run at about 40 kilometres an hour, if they have to. Their burrows may be 30 metres long and half a metre high, so they protect them from heat, rain and, above all, from bushfires. A wombat can dig about two metres of burrow in one night."

Tom continued, "They're lucky. People lose their homes and sometimes they die in bushfires, too. We have a boy in our class who used to live in Duffy, Canberra. A few years ago there were some really big bushfires down there. Well, he told us that one afternoon he was in the car with his mom going to the shopping mall, when they heard on the radio that fires had started in their area. The sky suddenly became grey with smoke. They saw fire engines and suddenly the sun disappeared and it got dark. They turned round and drove back home again, and from the car they saw the orange glow of burning trees in the distance. Then, not far away there was a loud bang. Later they heard that a gas station had blown up. When they got home their dad was hosing down the house and garden, like lots of other people in the street. They took their animals from the yard into the house to keep them safe – including their parrot who never stopped talking. Dan said the most scary part was when the sky went black with smoke and the power went out in the middle of the afternoon. It was dark and they were really scared. They were lucky that the wind turned and the fires didn't reach their street, but half the kids in Dan's class lost their homes and some old people died – Dan's grandfather, too. Lots of people were evacuated from their houses, and Dan's grandfather had a heart attack because he was so scared about leaving his home. He died on the way to hospital."

"Oh, that's terrible," said Jeff, who had listened to every word that Tom had said without interrupting.

"Poor Dan," Alice said, who was obviously very moved by Tom's story. "The bushfires must be really scary. Can't the government do more to prevent them?"

"Well, we get bushfires all over in the south and right up the New South Wales coast, too. Some years are worse than others. It depends on how much it has rained, how high the temperatures climb and on the direction of the winds. But thousands of hectares of bushland are burnt and hundreds of homes. There are often 3000 firefighters working day and night. They even come in to help us from New Zealand, Canada and the US. It's a hard job. Sometimes they have to work for days without a break. There isn't much time for sleep, and it's dangerous, too."

"We've often seen bushfires on the news on TV back home. The fires seem to be around Christmas and New Year," said Alice.

"Yes, sometimes they start early in December and continue until February. It depends on the weather. Anyway, look, here we are! The Koala Park. Everybody out! Jeff and Alice, you're going to love this."

*

Tom and Jeff went on ahead while Uncle Bill bought the tickets for the four of them. Aunt Sarah had to go to work and Rachel wasn't with them because she had gone riding with Shannon – of course. But Alice didn't really mind, and after all, Rachel must have seen hundreds of koalas and kangaroos.

At the moment Alice was excited about the animals she was going to see. She felt such a thrill when she saw her first koalas.

"Oh, look! There's a joey on its mother's back!" she called out with delight.

"Hey! How do you know that we call babies joeys?" asked Tom in surprise. It was usually Jeff who had all the information about Australia, not Alice. Alice thought about Cam. He had told her about joeys and lots of other things about koalas. She just smiled and said, "Cam."

"Cam? Who's Cam?" Jeff wanted to know, curious as ever. But Tom continued, "They're cute, aren't they? And this little guy is very cute – or is it a "she"? Males are a bit bigger than females and they can be up to fifty per cent heavier than females, but you can't really tell with joeys."

Alice tried to take photographs, but it wasn't easy. Either the koalas were half hidden behind the eucalyptus leaves or they were asleep, sitting on the branch of a tree. "Hey, we're lucky. The koala show is going to start in a few minutes," said Bill.

"What do they do, dance?" asked Jeff, trying to be funny.

"Ha ha," answered Alice. "That isn't funny, Jeff. Let's just wait and see, shall we?" In the meantime, an audience of at least thirty people had gathered near the main koala yard and a few minutes later a young red-haired woman appeared with a very cute koala on her arm.

"G'day, everybody, and welcome to Billabong. My name is Kate and this little guy here is called Buffalo Bill, but everybody calls him Billy. First I'm going to tell you a bit

about Billy and his mates, then you can ask questions, and afterwards you can come up and pat him and take photos."

Alice, Jeff and Tom managed to get a place in the front row, quite close to Kate and Billy. Kate told her audience a lot of very interesting koala facts which were all new to Jeff. Alice found that she knew quite a lot already from Cameron, but she listened with interest.

They found out that "koala" is an Aboriginal word that means "doesn't drink". Koalas eat leaves from eucalyptus or "gum" trees, so that's why they always smell of cough sweets.

A eucalyptus leaf contains 50% water, so koalas don't usually need to drink extra water. There are about 600 different types of eucalyptus leaves in different parts of Australia, but koalas eat only 50 to 60 of them. Of the kinds that grow in any one area, a koala will eat only five or six. Kate also said that koalas eat for around four hours each day and sleep for almost twenty. They are great climbers, but they only climb one

per cent of the time. Jeff's comment to this was "Wow! What a great life! Just eating and sleeping. Why can't I be a koala?"

"Hey, that's a good idea!" shouted Alice, laughing. "It would be a lot quieter at home!"

The young visitors also learnt that koalas can't see very well, so they rely mostly on their ears and nose. They can run quite quickly for a short distance, and they can also swim if they have to, but they live in the trees, not on the ground. They don't have much energy because all they eat is gum leaves, so you see them eating, sleeping or resting in trees most of the time. That's how they save their energy.

In the question time after Kate's talk Jeff said, "Hi, my name's Jeff. I have a question. What do joeys look like when they're born, and when are they fully grown?"

Kate answered, "Hi, you're from the UK, right? You've come a long way to visit our koalas, Jeff. Well, here's your answer. Koala joeys look kind of funny at birth. They're pink, they're blind, and they're only about two centimetres long, as big as a jelly bean, and they weigh less than half a gram. Their eyes open when they're about 22 weeks old. They live in their mother's pouch and drink her milk for the first few months. Then, at about six months, they get their teeth and they start to come out of the pouch. That's when they try their first gum leaves. At eight months the joey is too big for its mother's pouch, so it rides on her back. But joeys don't leave their moms until they're about a year old. Then they have to look after themselves. But life for young koalas isn't always easy. It can be dangerous when they're on the ground because sometimes dogs attack them."

"Dogs? How come? There aren't many dogs in eucalyptus forests," Jeff interrupted.

"That's right, Jeff," Kate continued. The biggest problem for koalas is that in many areas they are losing their habitat. Gum trees provide food and homes for koalas, but the trees they live in are often cut down to build roads and houses, so sometimes koalas find themselves in trees in people's yards. If there's a dog, it might easily attack the koala. Another problem is that koalas often get hit by cars when they cross the road to look for new trees."

Next someone in the audience asked how long koalas usually live. "Well, in the wild they probably live about ten to twelve years, but when they live in animal parks, where they're protected and fed well, they can live for twelve to fifteen years," was Kate's answer.

*

After the show, the patting and the photographs, Jeff wanted to be the first to see a kangaroo, so he hurried off with Tom to find them. Alice didn't want to leave the koalas, but she

Kangaroo

followed after a while with Uncle Bill. Jeff loved the kangaroos, especially the cute babies which are also called "joeys". Tom explained that the kangaroos in New South Wales were Eastern Greys. They live in the east of Australia, usually in groups of ten or more. There are also Red Kangaroos, but they are bigger and not so pretty as the Eastern Greys. They live more in the outback, Tom said.

"Hey, you know a lot about kangaroos. Tell me more," Jeff went on.

"Well, they're fast. Greys can travel at a speed of up to 60 kilometres per hour," said Tom. "In fact, the record is 64 kilometres per hour, held by a female Eastern Grey."

"Wow, that's fast. And how far can they jump?" Jeff wanted to know.

"Well, a friend told me that the record is 13.5 metres, and a Grey once jumped over a fence that was 2.44 metres high."

"Cool," replied Jeff, wanting to know more. And what about the joeys when they're born?"

"Oh, they're born after 36 days. They weigh under one gram and are pink, without hair. They live in their mother's pouch until they're about 11 months old, but they don't live without their moms until they're about 18 months. An adult male Eastern Grey may weigh up to 66 kilos, females only about half that much. But you should see the males boxing. That's fun."

"Boxing?" said Alice wanting to know why.

"Sure. They box and wrestle to test who's the top kangaroo in the mob," explained Tom.

"That sounds a bit like some kids at school," was Alice's comment. Jeff and Tom nodded in agreement.

"Well, come on. Let's move on," said Tom. "We can come back to the kangaroos again later if you want. Who wants to see the new reptile house?"

Saltwater Crocodile

Desert Death Adder

Freshwater Crocodile

Inland Taipan

"Me!" shouted Jeff enthusiastically. "I want to see the most poisonous snakes, the man-eating crocodiles and the deadly spiders."

"Well, I'll go back to the koalas with Uncle Bill," said Alice, who had no intention of looking at killer snakes. In fact, she hoped that she would never ever see any snakes.

In the new reptile house, Tom told Jeff that there are about 140 different kinds of snakes in Australia. Tom showed Jeff an inland taipan, the most poisonous land snake in the world. He told him that its bite is at least twenty times more poisonous than the bite of an Indian cobra.

"Just imagine," said Tom, "the poison from a single bite might be strong enough to kill about 250,000 mice."

"Wow," was Jeff's only comment. He suddenly seemed to feel a lot of respect for the snake as he took a step back from the taipan's glass cage. Then he said, "I bet Alice will be glad she didn't come with us. I must tell her all the details. She'll be really scared. Cool."

Chapter 8 A day to remember

Jeff had soon made new friends. On the evening of the welcome barbecue, a boy called Mark had invited him to his house to see a kangaroo joey who had lost its mum. Mark's mum was raising the joey with a bottle.

A few days days later, Mark phoned Jeff and asked him if he would like to go to his house on the next day to see the joey. Jeff was very pleased about that and he was thrilled at the idea of hand-feeding a baby kangaroo. He asked Uncle Bill if he could go to Mark's on Tom's bike. Tom had to help his dad so he couldn't go with Jeff. Aunt Sarah didn't think it was such a good idea for Jeff to cycle around Port on his own, so she suggested that Alice should go with him and that she could take her bike. It was better than Rachel's bike because it had a bigger basket. Alice said she would like to go with Jeff because on that day Rachel was going riding with Shannon. Rachel had asked Alice if she would like to go with them, but Alice knew that she would be alone for most of the day.

"Here's a cut lunch to take with you. And maybe you should take a pullover or a jacket. It's going to be windy later. Did Mark tell you exactly how to get to his house?" went on Aunt Sarah, sounding more and more like their own mother. "And here's some water and some fruit. Ride carefully and please don't be back too late. Do you have our telephone number in case you need to call us?"

"Yes, Aunt Sarah. Thanks. We've got everything now. It isn't far and we won't get lost. Jeff knows the way – and we won't be back late," promised Alice.

*

They enjoyed the ride through Port Macquarie. Alice found cycling in the cool breeze very pleasant. Jeff took the lead and rode in front. They rode on the cycle paths and looked at the nice houses and holiday apartments on the way. "This really is a great place for a holiday," said Jeff.

Jeff was really looking forward to feeding the baby kangaroo. In the evenings he wrote e-mails to his friends in London to tell them about the exciting things he had done. What would they say when they knew that he had fed a baby kangaroo with a bottle? That was something that absolutely nobody in his school class had done.

As they were just riding onto Ocean Drive, Alice called to Jeff, "Hey, my shoelace is undone. I'll have to stop for a minute, and I think there's a stone in my shoe, too. It hurts. You can have a sandwich while you're waiting for me. Here they are. Catch!" Jeff rode on a little, then stopped to eat a sandwich and wait for Alice on the cycle path.

Alice got off her bike and moved it away from the cycle path into some bushes. She sat down on the dry grass to tie her shoelace – when suddenly she heard a strange sound from behind one of the bushes. She felt scared. After all, in Australia a noise from behind a bush could mean a poisonous snake or some other dangerous animal. All kinds of frightening thoughts went through her mind. She quickly put on her right shoe and stood up. Slowly and quietly, her heart beating loudly, she walked up to the bush and …

"Oh no! Jeff! Jeff! Come quickly! Look!"

Jeff heard that Alice's voice was strangely anxious, so he dropped his bike at the side of the cycle path and ran quickly towards the bushes. On the grass there lay a young koala, injured and bleeding …

Shocked at their discovery, Alice and Jeff got down on their knees and looked at the young koala's head where there was a deep wound. His eye was bleeding and he was shivering.

"Poor thing. I think he's breathing, but he can't move. He must have been hit by a car and managed to get off the road into the bushes," said Jeff .

Alice went on with tears in her eyes, "We've got to help him. But how?"

"Don't panic, Al. I'm here, OK?" Jeff said in a very calm and quiet manner. "Now listen. We'll take him to the Koala Hospital. It's in Lord Street, on the Macquarie Nature Reserve. I don't think it's far from here. Let's look at the map. Look, we're about here, so it's just up Lake Road, then right into Hill Street, down Lord Street and then we're at the hospital. It won't take us long to get there. Let's wrap him in my pullover and your jacket and we'll put him in your basket. Come on, hurry. There's no time to lose."

"But what if he dies on the way there?" cried Alice in a state of shock. "I'm scared, Jeff."

"That's why we have to take him straightaway. Come on Alice, lift him up with me. Come on. You can do it."

Very carefully they wrapped the little koala in Jeff's pullover and very gently lifted him into the bicycle basket. Alice covered him with her jacket. For once Alice was very glad that Jeff knew so much. He knew there was a koala hospital in Port Macquarie and he knew where it was and how to get there. Suddenly she realised that her little brother was, in fact, quite grown-up. He knew what to do. He was calm and sensible. He took command where Alice panicked. She felt safe with him. She said through her tears, "Jeff, I'll never say that you're a know-all again."

"Forget it, sis. You found him. He's your koala. He's lucky that you had to tie your shoelace right next to the bush where he was lying. What a coincidence! Just imagine, perhaps nobody would have found him. Come on. Let's get him to the hospital. Quickly!"

*

Jeff led the way and Alice followed with the furry, little bundle in her bicycle basket. Jeff was right again, it wasn't far to the Koala Hospital. It was set in the Macquarie Nature Reserve, a large green area of eucalypt forest. They soon found the low white buildings of the hospital and the yards outside. It was so quiet and peaceful there. Alice looked for someone to ask and saw a lady in one of the koala yards.

"Hello. We've just found an injured koala on the roadside. I've got him in my basket. He's hurt but we think he's still breathing,"Alice managed to say hurriedly in an anxious voice.

"Oh dear. He was probably hit by a car. He was lucky that you found him. Let's hope the injuries aren't too serious. Come on, we'll take him to our supervisor. She'll examine him and find out how bad his injuries are," said the lady in a kind voice, taking the koala very carefully out of the basket. "My name's Joy."

"And we're Alice and Jeff." They followed Joy into the hospital. She took the koala into a treatment room. The supervisor, another very nice lady called Kelly, joined them and spoke a few encouraging words. Alice told her where they had found the koala. In fact, Kelly wasn't surprised that the accident had happened on Ocean Drive, one of the two main streets in Port. Kelly suggested that Alice and Jeff should wait outside until she had examined the little koala with one of her helpers.

"Is he going to be OK?" said Alice to Jeff, trying hard to hold back her tears. She was still shaken.

"We'll just have to wait and see," he replied. "We did all we could, sis."

"You were brilliant, Jeff. I'll never forget it," Alice said, touching him gently on his cheek. I'm so lucky to have a brother like you – a little know-all..."

While they were waiting, they watched the koalas sleeping or resting in the recovery yards. Some seemed to be quite young. In one yard there was a mother with a joey on her back. Alice and Jeff spoke to Joy, who was still in one of the yards. She told them a lot about the work at the hospital and answered their questions. Alice was very interested. They found out that the hospital was run mainly by volunteers. The helpers clean the yards and change the leaves so that the little patients always have fresh food. They put fresh water in the yards, too, even though koalas don't drink much. The koalas get treatment and medication. Some of the koalas are hand-fed with a special high-protein milk formula. Some koalas are in an intensive care unit (ICU) before they go into a recovery yard.

Jeff and Alice found out that at 3 pm there's also the daily "feed, walk and talk" programme. A volunteer guide takes visitors round the outside yards and tells them about the koala patients, why they are in the hospital and how they are being treated. Alice said that she would definitely like to be there for the talk.

When Kelly called Alice and Jeff back in after she had examined their koala, she told them that he was a young male, about one and a half years old. He had a head wound, his right eye was hurt and he most probably had a broken jaw. They would have to take X-rays to see if he had internal injuries, and the vet would look at him as soon as he could. In the meantime Kelly had given the koala some medication to take away the pain. Kelly said he was sleeping now in the ICU and they could go and see him if they wanted to – and of course they wanted to.

As the koala lay there so peacefully, Alice knew that this little fellow would always be very special to her. But just how long would "always" be? The koala was badly hurt. Would he survive?

When they left the hospital Alice asked Kelly, "Can we come again tomorrow, please?"

"Of course you can," was her answer. "You'll always be welcome here. You can come any time. Oh, and think about a name for your koala. What would you like to call him?"

"How about Lucky Luke or Coca Koala?" said Jeff without much thought.

"Well, our little patients are sometimes named after the person who finds them or helps them. And the name often has to do with the place where the koala was found. For example, We've got a female koala called Ocean Therese, found on Ocean Drive by a lady called Therese."

"Oh, I see. Then it's easy. Alice found him on Ocean Drive, too, so we could call him Ocean Alice. But he's a male, so what about Ocean Al? What do you think, sis?"

"Well, you know I don't like you to call me Al, but I think it's a good name for our koala. Well done, Jeff. Is it OK, Kelly? Can we call him Ocean Al?"

"Sure you can. Ocean Al it is," was Kelly's answer.

*

Alice and Jeff cycled home as fast as they could to tell the news to their aunt and uncle and cousins. Jeff called Mark and explained why they hadn't been to visit the kangaroo joey. Everybody was very enthusiastic and thought that Alice and Jeff had done a really good job. Alice was worried about the little koala and thought about him all the time. That evening both Alice and Jeff wrote very interesting e-mails to their friends in London about Ocean Al and the Koala Hospital. As Alice lay in bed, she thought about the koala for a long time. Then suddenly she found herself thinking about Cameron. She wondered if maybe he would like to hear about the koala, too …

Chapter 9 Decisions

The next day Alice got up earlier than usual. She hadn't slept very well, but she was anxious to hear how Ocean Al had been in the night. Was he still alive?

Uncle Bill had planned to go fishing with Tom and Jeff that day, so Alice would go to the hospital alone. Thanks to Jeff she knew the way. She had a quick breakfast, then she set off on Aunt Sarah's bike.

Kelly told Alice that Ocean Al was sleeping quietly and she could see him. Alice was relieved that he had made it through the night. His head wound had been bathed and treated. Kelly also said that Phil, the vet, was going to examine him in his practice that same morning. Phil would take X-rays and then decide if the koala needed an operation.

Outside, the volunteers had already started their work. Alice was very interested in what they were doing, so she went up to them and asked lots of questions. Alice was usually shy, but she forgot her shyness. Some of the volunteers were young girls, not much older than she was. One girl, Heike, was a student from Germany, who was spending four weeks of the Christmas holiday in Port as an overseas volunteer. She was cleaning one of the yards and putting fresh leaves in the leaf container. She said that next she was going to hand-feed a young koala with protein formula for the first time. She said Alice could watch if she wanted. Alice wished so much that she could do it herself.

The time seemed to pass slowly as Alice waited for Kelly to return from the vet's. What would the vet say? What would he find on the X-rays? Would the koala need an operation?

Would the vet be able to save his life? Alice felt nervous. She felt the same bond to the little koala as she had done to Chico, when she had found him and taken him home. Until Kelly's return Alice spent the time talking to the volunteers and watching the koalas in the yards. She knew all their names now. She hoped that her koala would soon be in a recovery yard, too.

At last Kelly was back with Ocean Al, who was sleeping in her arms. Kelly took him into the ICU again. Then she told Alice that he needed an operation on his lower jaw. It was broken and if it didn't heal properly, he wouldn't be able to chew leaves. This meant that he would starve.

"A lower jaw isn't easy to repair. The upper and lower teeth must fit together so that the koala can chew properly," explained Kelly. "If he can't chew leaves, he'll die."

Kelly added that Phil and another vet, Ben, who was a specialist for jaw operations, would operate in two or three days, as soon as Ocean Al was strong enough for the anaesthetic. Until then he would go into intensive home care with an experienced carer called Barbara. She would feed him with protein formula, give him all the medical help he needed and lots of attention, too.

*

That evening Alice told the news to all the family. She phoned her parents in Sydney, too. Everybody was anxious to hear about the little koala, who was the main topic of conversation. Rachel had been riding with Shannon again, but nobody was very interested in hearing about that.

Alice spent the next two days either at the hospital or at Barbara's house with Ocean Al. Jeff went with her, but he didn't stay as long as Alice did. She never lost interest in her sick koala. From Barbara Alice learnt a lot about koalas and about how to care for them. Barbara told her about the dangers for koalas and about the diseases which they often have. She said that the hospital worked closely together with Sydney University, as Kelly was involved in several research projects.

Barbara told Alice stories of koalas who were hurt in bushfires. She said most koalas didn't survive. Hundreds or even thousands lost their lives. Some had very bad burns and had to stay at the hospital for a year or longer before they could be released into the wild again. Many became blind. Some were even permanent patients who had to stay at the hospital until they died. About 250 koalas were treated at the hospital every year.

Barbara also told Alice that the hospital costs were very high, about $140,000 per year, mainly for medical bills and supplies, bills for the leaf truck, telephone, computers, etc. Alice realised that the hospital relied on donations and she decided immediately that she would support the *Adopt A Koala* programme from her pocket money. Alice knew that her parents would help, too.

And she had another idea. She had decided to ask Kelly if she could be a hospital volunteer for the rest of the holidays. She wanted to do something useful with her time – and what could be better than helping sick animals?

Alice was afraid that perhaps Kelly would not take her seriously, but in fact she was pleased and she agreed immediately. Alice could start the next morning and join the volunteers on the first shift from 7.30 to 12 o'clock. Alice was excited. She couldn't do much for Ocean Al, but she would feel better if she could help the other koalas at the hospital. Kelly said that if she wished, she could sometimes help out in the hospital souvenir shop in the afternoons, too. It would be her first job, and Alice was determined to do it well. In fact, she felt quite proud of herself.

Later that afternoon there was an unexpected phone call for Alice.

"Hi, Alice. Remember me?" said a male voice at the other end.

Yes, indeed. Alice remembered the caller very well. It was Cam.

"How about a visit to the best ice cream place in town?" he said cheerfully. "I'm sure there's lots to talk about. Bring your little brother, too. It's my treat."

"Great. Thank you, and I'm sure Jeff will come, too. He loves ice cream. And yes, there really is lots to talk about," Alice said happily. Cam said he would pick them up in ten minutes and they could cycle into town together. As she put down the phone, she felt her heart beating loudly. Alice thought how nice it was of Cam to invite Jeff, too. Alice was excited – and there were those butterflies in her stomach again ... But what should she say to Jeff? He didn't know anything about Cam.

"Who's Cam," was the first question – which Alice was expecting. "Is he your boyfriend?"

"No, he isn't my boyfriend," Alice answered. He's just a nice boy I know. He's Shannon's brother. You know, Rachel's best friend. I met him at her party a few evenings ago. He knows a lot about animals."

"Well, whether he is your boyfriend or he isn't, sure I'll go for an ice cream with him. It isn't time for supper yet. I'll tell Aunt Sarah we're going."

Alice quickly combed her hair and put on a bit of lip gloss. Suddenly she wanted to look her best. As Cam came cycling down the road Jeff said, "Hey, is that him, sis? He looks OK."

"Shhh!" replied Alice. "Be quiet, he'll hear you."

"So what?" was Jeff's reaction. "Girls!"

"Oh, so you're Cameron. Alice talks about you all the time. Are you her boyfriend?" began Jeff in his all too direct manner. Alice was so embarrassed. How could Jeff do that to her? "That's not true. You'll have to excuse my brother. He's a chatterbox," Alice said, trying to save the situation.

"I like people who say what they think," laughed Cameron. "You're OK, Jeff. Right. Shall we go? Shall I take the lead?"

"No, I can take the lead, Cam. We've been to the ice cream place before with Uncle Bill. I know where it is," was Jeff's answer.

Jeff did know the way, and they were soon there. They parked their bikes and sat down at a corner table outside. Alice's heart was beating fast again for some reason – and it wasn't the bike ride or the heat ...

Jeff had the biggest ice cream that he had ever eaten. Alice was glad that he was busy with the ice cream because it meant that he wouldn't talk as much as usual. There was lots to talk about, but the koala rescue, explained in all details very dramatically by Jeff, was the focus of attention. Alice told Cam that she was very worried about the operation. Ocean Al was weak and maybe had internal injuries, too. Cam told her that the little guy was in very capable hands, and that the hospital saved so many koalas every year. Alice also told Cam that she was going to start there as a volunteer on the next day. He looked at her and said, "That's really great, Alice. I admire you."

It wasn't just what Cam said, but it was the way he said it – and the way he looked at her when he said it. Alice now knew that not only her little koala was special to her ... But Cam? He was such a nice person, so interesting, and so good-looking, a bit older, too. He must surely have a girl-friend. He couldn't be interested in Alice. He hadn't mentioned any girls, but Alice didn't know him very well yet. Maybe his girlfriend had gone on holiday or maybe she was doing a holiday job somewhere else and wasn't in Port at the time. Alice decided that Cam was just being very friendly to the English visitors. Perhaps he just enjoyed hearing their English accent. Perhaps people from London reminded him of his stay there. Perhaps he didn't have much else to do at the moment.

On the way back home, Jeff took the lead again, happily whistling the tune of "Waltzing Matilda". He was looking forward to playing football with Tom before supper. Cam and Alice rode behind Jeff, side by side. On the way home Cam told Alice that he was helping out in his dad's town office in the holidays, but only in the mornings. He asked her if he could call in at the hospital after work the next day to hear how her koala was. Alice said she would be very glad of his support. Cam loved animals. She was sure that he was only interested in the koala. Perhaps she would find out the next day ...

Chapter 10 New directions

The big day had arrived, the day when Phil and Ben were going to operate on Ocean Al. Alice hadn't slept very well, so she felt tired and nervous at breakfast. Jeff wanted to go to the vet's with her – to hold her hand, he said. Kelly said they could wait in the waiting room until the operation was over. Barbara would also be there. The vets, Phil and Ben, were already getting everything ready in the operating room, assisted by two vet nurses. Then Barbara arrived, carrying Ocean Al in a warm blanket. She stopped to let Alice and Jeff stroke him.

"Hi, little Al," said Alice gently with tears in her eyes. "Make sure you get well again, OK?" He looked so helpless, so fragile. Alice wished so much that she could do something to help him. Then Barbara gave him to one of the vet nurses, who took him into the operating room and closed the door.

In the next one and a half hours time seemed to stand still for Alice. The atmosphere was tense. She walked up and down and asked Barbara lots of questions about the operation. Barbara explained that Ben and Phil would put a metal plate into the koala's lower jaw. But it was a difficult operation. Jeff tried to calm Alice down. "Don't worry, Alice. Phil and Ben know what they're doing. They've done this kind of operation before. We just have to hope that little Al is strong enough."

"Yes, that's the problem – and let's hope that he hasn't got any serious internal injuries," Alice added. "He will be OK, won't he, Barbara?"

"Well, he should be OK if there aren't any unexpected complications. Every operation of this kind is dangerous because you don't know how the koala will react to the anaesthetic. But he's in good hands. We'll just have to wait and see." Alice walked up and down again, and again...

After what seemed like a week, the door of the operating room opened. Alice and Jeff stood up together and looked at Phil with open mouths, waiting for his news. Alice held her breath.

Phil went up to them and said, "Well, we had an unexpected problem – and for a moment we thought we were going to lose him. But he's OK now. The work on his jaw went well, but it's too early to say much more. We're going to keep him here until he wakes up, then Barbara will take him home again until he's stronger. You can help her if you like, Alice. I'm sure she will show you how to feed him and how to treat his head wound. With a bit of luck he'll soon be back in the hospital in the recovery yards. By the way, he was lucky to have good friends like you. He was very weak and he wouldn't have survived if you hadn't got him to the hospital so quickly. You gave him his life back."

Alice and Jeff smiled with relief. Alice had tears in her eyes – but this time they were tears of joy.

Just then there was an unexpected visitor to the vet's surgery.

"Hi, Alice. How did it go? I just finished work, so I came right over." It was Cam. Alice's smiling face told him that the news was good. "I guess Ocean Al made it," he said with a big smile. That's really fantastic. Ben and Phil are great vets."

"I can't tell you how happy and relieved we are. I must go home and tell my aunt and uncle and phone my parents.

Barbara, can I come to see Al this afternoon? I'd love to help you with him – if I can."
"No worries, Alice. Come when you want. You go home now and tell everyone the good news," Barbara said.

*

On the way home, Cam invited Alice and Jeff to a barbecue at his house that evening – to celebrate the good news, he said. This time Alice didn't hesitate. She accepted the invitation with a smile. She felt good about herself and her situation – and she knew that Shannon wouldn't be a problem any more. Shannon was Cam's sister, so she couldn't be all that bad, could she? After all, Rachel was Shannon's best friend, and suddenly a cousin from England appears and expects to have all Rachel's attention. Had Alice perhaps been a little jealous? A little unfair even? "Try and see it from Shannon's point of view, Alice," she thought to herself. "Shannon sometimes behaves like a spoilt little rich girl – but she must have her good points because Rachel likes her. Everybody deserves a second chance, Shannon, too."
Alice spent time with Barbara and little Ocean Al before she went to the barbecue. She arrived when most of the other guests were already there, but this time she didn't mind making her entrance alone. She knew that she had friends there, Trish, Jane, Rachel, Cam ...
What Alice didn't know was, in fact, exactly how many new friends she now had. Everyone had heard about the koala rescue from Cam or Rachel, and everyone knew that Alice was working as a volunteer at the Koala Hospital. They respected her for that. Everybody wanted to hear about little Al. Suddenly Alice had become a very popular person,

and for the first time in her life she found herself in the middle of a group of boys ...

Shannon came over to her and said, "Hi Alice. I've heard all about Ocean Al from Cam and that you're working at the Koala Hospital. We all think it's great that you're helping to look after our animals. It's a really Australian thing to do. You're one of us now." Then she whispered to Alice, "By the way, don't tell him I said so, but Cam talks about you all the time..." Alice's face turned a deep red.

"Hey, sis. It's great here. Pool parties are cool. Cam's invited me to come again tomorrow after he finishes work. He's going to show me his model planes. He says I can bring you, too – if you want to come. But I expect you'll be at Barbara's after your shift. Cam said something about going to the cinema in the evening, too – if you want to come."

*

For the rest of the holidays Alice worked at the Koala Hospital, even at the weekends. Everybody there liked her quiet, cheerful manner. She was very good with the animals and always friendly and helpful. Through her work she quickly became more outgoing, more self-confident, more independent. She didn't feel like a tourist any more. She felt that she was now part of something, something very Australian.

Alice's life now seemed to have a totally new focus. She had a job which she loved, which made her feel useful and needed. She had friends at the hospital and at home. She had a koala which was named after her – and she had Cam. Above all, she had a direction for the future. She knew what she wanted to do with her life – and she knew where she wanted to do it.

The day before her parents drove up to Port to take her and Jeff back to Sydney, she wrote an e-mail to Ann and Lucy: "... It's really great here. I don't know why I was so negative about everything at first. Sydney will be a new challenge, but I feel good about going there now. I'm even looking forward to school. We'll be in Port for the next holidays, I'm sure, perhaps even some weekends – you can fly to Port Macquarie from Sydney. I have to visit little Al as often as I can – and Cam, too. I think I know what I want to do now. I'd like to study veterinary medicine at Sydney University and become a vet – perhaps here in Port Macquarie. Who knows?

By the way, Cam gave me a leaving present today. He said it would remind me of my first stay in Port – as if I could ever forget. It's a little silver koala ...

You must come and visit me soon. You'll really like it here, you'll see ..."

Vocabulary

Chapter 1

bare [beə] nackt, leer
(to) **look forward to** sth sich auf etw. freuen
experience [ɪk'spɪəriəns] Erfahrung
(to) **disappear** verschwinden
enthusiastically [ɪnˌθju:zi'æstɪkli] begeistert
headphones Kopfhörer
(to) be **homesick** Heimweh haben
guide book Reiseführer
population Bevölkerung
greedy ['gri:di] gierig
It's a deal! Abgemacht!
on time pünktlich
know-all ['nəʊ ɔ:l] Besserwisser
enthusiasm [ɪn'θju:ziæzəm] Begeisterung
ferry Fähre
(to) **exhaust** [ɪg'zɔ:st] erschöpfen
sights Sehenswürdigkeiten

Chapter 2

cheerful fröhlich
(to) **bet** wetten
(to) **complain** klagen
forehead ['fɔ:hed] Stirn
(to) be **bothered** sich die Mühe machen
poisonous ['pɔɪzənəs] giftig
deadly tödlich
jellyfish Qualle
shark Hai
average ['ævərɪdʒ] durchschnittlich
degree Grad
mood Laune (*Gemütslage*)
scenery ['si:nəri] Landschaft
(to) **depend on** sth von etw. abhängen
roguish ['rəʊgɪʃ] schelmisch
air conditioning Klimaanlage
(to) **moan** stöhnen
remains Reste
runny geschmolzen
disappointed enttäuscht
envy ['envi] Neid
plenty viel
(to) **get lost** sich verfahren
surroundings Umgebung
in a bad mood schlecht gelaunt
(to) **chuckle** kichern
(to) **scratch** kratzen
rest area ['rest ˌeəriə] Raststätte
eucalyptus / eucalypt [ˌju:kə'lɪptəs / ˌju:kə'lɪpt] Eukalyptus
damage ['dæmɪdʒ] Schäden
(to) **hop** hüpfen

Chapter 3

fair dinkum (*AUS*) echt
genuine ['dʒenjuɪn] echt
(to) **be keen on** sth etw. unbedingt wollen
cookies Kekse
nosy neugierig

area Stadtgebiet
stacked aufgestapelt
neatly ordentlich
string Bindfaden
curious ['kjʊəriəs] neugierig
(to) **unload** ausladen
(to) **change the subject** das Thema wechseln
no worries kein Problem
uncomfortable unbehaglich
on show zur Schau gestellt
outgoing kontaktfreudig
self-confident selbstbewusst
gentle sanft(mütig)
sensitive ['sensətɪv] sensibel
(to) **value** schätzen
stray Streuner
bond Bindung
(to) **treat** behandeln
(to) **deserve** verdienen
melancholy ['melənkəli] melancholisch
impression Eindruck

Chapter 4

Aboriginal people [ˌæbə'rɪdʒənl] Ureinwohner Australiens
impressed beeindruckt
inhabitants Einwohner
(to) **encourage** [ɪn'kʌrɪdʒ] ermutigen
(to) **hire** ['haɪə] mieten
(to) **interrupt** unterbrechen
(to) **sample** *hier*: probieren
cheeky frech
relieved erleichtert
flavour Geschmacksrichtung
courthouse Gerichtsgebäude
gift Geschenk
sunscreen Sonnencreme
ozone hole ['əʊzəʊn] Ozonloch
sleeve Ärmel
stinger Qualle
box jellyfish Würfelqualle
dessert [dɪ'zɜːt] Nachspeise
patio ['pætiəʊ] Terrasse
(to) **decorate** schmücken
Chinese lanterns Lampions
apron ['eɪprən] Küchenschürze

Chapter 5

(to) **protest** [prə'test] protestieren
dying to do sth etwas unbedingt tun wollen
hairslide Haarspange
smart klug
pick (freie) Wahl
(to) **embarrass** [ɪm'bærəs] in Verlegenheit bringen
conservative [kən'sɜːvətɪv] konservativ, bieder
apart from außer, abgesehen von
likely wahrscheinlich
(to) **judge** beurteilen
slim schlank
bubbly sprudelnd, quirlig
surf Brandung
(to) **complain** sich beklagen
sincere [sɪn'sɪə] aufrichtig
spontaneously [spɒn'teɪniəsli] spontan
delight Entzücken
(to) **draw** anziehen
magnet ['mægnət] Magnet
crowd Clique

Chapter 6

boardwalk Holzsteg
canopy ['kænəpi] Baldachin, *hier*: Laub- / Blätterdach
jet skiers ['dʒet ˌskiːəz] Jet Ski-Fahrer (*Jet Ski = motorbetriebenes Wasserfahrzeug, das aussieht wie ein Motorroller ohne Räder*)
gates Tor
IT company (IT = information technology) *Firma für Informationstechnologie*
fountain Springbrunnen
bench Sitzbank
(to) **glitter** glitzern
turquoise ['tɜːkwɔɪz] türkis
(to) **dangle** baumeln lassen
stunning umwerfend
heel (Schuh)Absatz
superficial [ˌsuːpə'fɪʃl] oberflächlich
(to) **gather** ['gæðə] sich versammeln
cell phone Handy
immediately [ɪ'miːdiətli] sofort, direkt
vet Tierarzt
attention Aufmerksamkeit
jealous ['dʒeləs] eifersüchtig
stay Aufenthalt
obviously offensichtlich
sensible ['sensəbl] vernünftig

Chapter 7

cuddly knuddelig
keeper Tierpfleger/-in
(to) **pat** tätscheln, streicheln
spark Funke
flash of lightning Blitz(schlag)
(to) **store** lagern
deliberately[dɪ'lɪbərətli] vorsätzlich
ground Boden, Erde
cute [kjuːt] niedlich
fellow Kerl
brain Gehirn
burrow ['bʌrəʊ] Bau
glow Leuchten
gas station Tankstelle
(to) **hose** sth **down** etw. mit Schlauch abspritzen
yard *hier*: Garten
power Strom
heart attack Herzanfall
(to) **prevent** verhindern
thrill Erregung
joey ['dʒəʊi] junger Koala / junges Känguruh
audience Publikum
yard *hier*: Gehege
mate Kamerad
cough sweets ['kɒf swiːt] Hustenbonbons
(to) **rely on** sth sich auf etw. verlassen
jelly bean Gummibärchen
pouch Beutel
habitat ['hæbɪtæt] Lebensraum
(to) **wrestle** ['resl] ringen
mob Gruppe (*besonders Känguruhs*)

Chapter 8

(to) **raise** aufziehen
cut lunch belegte Brote
lead Führung
shoelace Schuhband

undone offen (*z. B. Schnürsenkel, Knopf, etc.*)
(to) **tie** binden
anxious ['æŋkʃəs] ängstlich
injured ['ɪndʒəd] verletzt
discovery Entdeckung
wound [wu:nd] Wunde
(to) **shiver** zittern
(to) **take command** die Führung übernehmen
coincidence [kəʊ'ɪnsɪdəns] Zufall
furry ['fɜ:ri] flauschig
peaceful friedlich
supervisor ['su:pəvaɪzə] Leiter/-in
(to) **examine** [ɪg'zæmɪn] untersuchen
treatment Behandlung
shaken aufgewühlt
recovery Genesung
medication Medizin
protein ['prəʊti:n] Eiweiß
formula Milchpulver
intensive care unit (ICU) Intensivstation
definitely ['defɪnətli] bestimmt
jaw [dʒɔ:] Kiefer
X-ray ['eks reɪ] Röntgenaufnahme
internal injuries innere Verletzungen
pain Schmerz
survive [sə'vaɪv] überleben

Chapter 9

(to) **be anxious** to do sth etw. unbedingt tun wollen
(to) **bathe** [beið] baden
container Behälter
bond (Ver)Bindung
(to) **heal** abheilen
(to) **chew** kauen
properly richtig
(to) **starve** verhungern
upper obere(r/s)
anaesthetic [ˌænəs'θetɪk] Betäubung
experienced erfahren
disease [dɪ'zi:z] Krankheit
research ['ri:sɜ:tʃ] Forschung
(to) **release** [rɪ'li:s] freisetzen
bills Rechnungen
supplies [sə'plaɪz] Vorräte
donation Geldspende
support unterstützen
determined [dɪ'tɜ:mɪnd] fest entschlossen
It´s my treat Ich lade dich ein
chatterbox Plappermaul
rescue ['reskju:] Rettung
capable ['keɪpəbl] fähig
(to) **admire** [əd'maɪə] bewundern
(to) **mention** ['menʃn] erwähnen
(to) **whistle** ['wɪsl] pfeifen
tune [tju:n] Melodie

Chapter 10

blanket ['blæŋkɪt] Decke
stroke streicheln
fragile ['frædʒaɪl] zerbrechlich
tense angespannt
breath [breθ] Atem
relief [rɪ'li:f] Erleichterung
joy Freude

surgery ['sɜːdʒəri] Sprechzimmer (*Arzt*)
(to) **make it** durchkommen
(to) **hesitate** zögern
attention Aufmerksamkeit
spoilt verwöhnt
independent [ˌɪndɪ'pendənt] selbstständig
challenge ['tʃæləndʒ] Herausforderung
leaving present Abschiedsgeschenk

Names and place names

Chapter 1
Alice ['ælɪs]
Jeff [dʒef]
Chico ['tʃɪkəʊ]
Heathrow Airport [ˌhi:θ'rəʊ 'eəpɔ:t]
Cathay Pacific [ˌkæθeɪ pə'sɪfɪk]
Victoria Peak [vɪkˌtɔ:rɪə 'pi:k]
Port Macquarie [ˌpɔ:t mə'kwɒri]
Sarah ['seərə]
Rachel ['reɪtʃəl]

Chapter 2
Lighthouse Beach [ˌlaɪthaʊs 'bi:tʃ]
Brisbane ['brɪzbən]
Bondi Beach [ˌbɒndaɪ 'bi:tʃ]

Chapter 3
Aussies ['ɒziz]

Chapter 4
Aboriginal [ˌæbə'rɪdʒənl]
Asia ['eɪʒə, 'eɪʃə]
Ayers Rock [ˌeəz 'rɒk]
Maritime Museum [ˌmærɪtaɪm mju'zi:əm]
Flynns Beach [ˌflɪnz 'bi:tʃ]
Oxley Beach [ˌɒksli 'bi:tʃ]
Lake Cathie [ˌleɪk 'kætaɪ]

Chapter 6
Sea Acres ['si: ˌeɪkəz]
Pancake Palace [ˌpænkeɪk 'pæləs]

Chapter 7
Duffy ['dʌfi]
Canberra ['kænbərə]

Chapter 8
Ocean Drive [ˌəʊʃn 'draɪv]
Ocean Therese [ˌəʊʃn tə'ri:z]

Questions and Activities

Chapter 1

1 Why doesn't Alice want to go to Australia? Give three reasons.

2 What information do we find about Hong Kong in this chapter? Write a short paragraph.

3 How do we know that Alice is already homesick? Find the places in the text which tell us this and write down the line numbers.

Chapter 2

1 What do we know about Jeff and Alice from this chapter? How are they different from each other? Describe Alice in a short paragraph. Then describe Jeff in a short paragraph.

2 Do you agree with Alice that Jeff is a know-all? Or is he simply bright (*aufgeweckt*) and interested?

3 Would you like to go to Australia with your family for three years? Why or why not? Give your reasons.

4 On the Internet find out about Sydney Opera House, Bondi Beach and Sydney Harbour Bridge. Write two or three sentences about each.

5 Would you like to do the Bridge Climb? Find information about the Climb on the Internet, then write your answer in a short paragraph.
Try: www.bridgeclimb.com

6 What do we find out about Port Macquarie from this chapter?

Chapter 3

1 Look at the illustration and describe Uncle Bill, Aunt Sarah, Rachel and Tom.
2 What are "fair dinkum Aussies"?
3 Why isn't Alice looking forward to the barbecue?
4 How do we know that Alice still has a negative attitude towards the new country? Find and write down the line numbers.
5 What else do we find out about the characters of Alice and Jeff in this chapter? Underline the adjectives which describe them best:
Jeff nosy · self-confident · tidy direct · gentle
Alice outspoken · sensitive · shy · outgoing · serious

Chapter 4

1 Look at a map of Australia and find the following: Canberra (the capital), Sydney, Brisbane, Melbourne, Darwin, Adelaide, Perth; Uluru (Ayers Rock), The Great Barrier Reef.
2 What do you remember about the size of Australia and its population?
3 What do we learn about the Aboriginal people of Australia? Use the Internet to find out more. Write two short paragraphs.
(Try: www.infoplease.com/spot/aboriginal1.html)
4 Why doesn't Alice want to go in the sea?
5 At the end of this chapter, Alice is not looking forward to the barbecue. What is she perhaps afraid of?

Chapter 5

1 Who is Shannon? What does she look like?
2 What impression do we get of her from this chapter?

3 Why doesn't Alice feel good about the invitation to Shannon's pool party?
4 Does Jeff enjoy the welcome barbecue? Why?

Chapter 6

1 Alice meets Cam at the pool party. Who is he? Why does Alice like to talk to him?
2 How does Cam seem to be different from his sister?
3 Cam tells Alice a lot about Australian animals and birds (ll. 25–28). Have you heard of any of them? Choose three from the list and find out about them from the Internet. (Try: www.australian-animals.net)

Chapter 7

1 On the way to Billabong Wildlife Park Uncle Bill and Tom tell Jeff and Alice a lot about bushfires. Write a summary of the main facts.
2 In this chapter we find out a lot of information about koalas and kangaroos. Choose either koalas or kangaroos and write down as many facts as you can in a few paragraphs.
3 What is the biggest problem for koalas?
4 What does Jeff find out from Tom about Australian snakes?
5 Do you like snakes? Say why or why not.

Chapter 8

1 Why does Jeff want to go to Mark's house?
2 What happens on the way?
3 Explain what Alice and Jeff do with the injured koala.
4 How does Alice see her brother now? Does she still think that he's a know-all?

5 Describe the work of the volunteers at the Koala Hospital.
6 How does Ocean Al get his name?

Chapter 9

1 What facts does Barbara tell Alice about the Koala Hospital?
2 Why was the operation on Ocean Al's jaw necessary?
3 What decision does Alice make in this chapter?

Chapter 10

1 Why was Alice so nervous before Ocean Al's operation?
2 What differences do we see in Alice in this chapter? How would you describe her now?
3 What do you think helped to change her attitude?
4 What are Alice's plans for the future?
5 Would you like to have a job working with animals? Write a short paragraph.

Group work/Project work

1 How do you think the story of Alice in Australia will continue? In groups, discuss what might happen and write down the best ideas. Then present your ideas in class.
2 Do a project about the Koala Hospital.
Find out more about the *Adopt A Koala* programme and include it in your project.
(Try: www.koalahospital.org.au)